Let's Start with the Kids

A Curriculum for Children with Parents in Prison

Copyright © 2010, Let's Start Inc.
All rights reserved.

Let's Start Inc.
1408 S. 10th Street
St. Louis, MO 63104
Phone: 314-241-2324
www.letsstart.org

Library of Congress Control Number: 2010937852
ISBN: 978-1-933370-98-9

Printed in the United States of America
10 11 12 13 14   5 4 3 2 1

Contents

Year 1

Year 2

Let's Start with the Kids

Year 1

Contents

Introduction

After twenty years' experience working with families impacted by addiction and incarceration, Let's Start, Inc. has made a commitment to helping women and their children who are coping with the effects of imprisonment. Let's Start is an organization led by and for formerly incarcerated women, which aims to break the cycle of incarceration in families *by using the personal experiences of its participants to support individual recovery, educate the community, and inform public policy*.

The impact of parental incarceration on children is often overlooked. Let's Start has developed a support process for elementary school–age children in response to the stress that the loss of a parent to prison and/or jail puts on young children. This process offers the children the opportunity to enhance their coping skills to better respond to the stress of parental incarceration, and also to share their experiences, thoughts, and feelings with their peers in a group setting. What follows is an overview of the current evidence about incarceration and its effects on families, an outline of the curriculum used during the group process, and evaluation measures used.

Purpose of the Handbook

This handbook is to provide a guide for the professionals working with children who have been impacted by parental incarceration, i.e. teachers, guidance counselors, social workers, therapists, and school administrators. The challenges faced by these children are unique and serious. Let's Start firmly believes that in order to mediate the risks of related issues, such as depression, social isolation, and criminal activity, children of incarcerated parents should be supported in developing effective coping skills and a healthy social network.

It is understood that due to organizational structure, staff goals, and/or clients' needs a degree of flexibility is necessary to provide services to children with an incarcerated parent. This handbook provides an overview of the process which Let's Start has found to be effective. It can be used as a guide for other organizations as well.

Understanding the Impact of Incarceration on Children

The number of children with an incarcerated parent has increased rapidly over the past sixteen years. The Bureau of Justice estimates that there was an 80 percent increase between 1991 and 2007 in the number of children with a parent in prison, with the number currently estimated at more than 1.7 million (Glaze & Maruschak, 2009). These numbers do not include children with parents in the city or county jail systems across the country. Although the state of Missouri has made significant strides in reducing the prison population, including a .07 percent decrease from 2006 to 2007 (Sabol & Couture, 2008), thousands of children are impacted by the incarceration of a primary caregiver each year.

As a result of parental incarceration, children are put at increased risk for a number of negative outcomes, and their unique needs often go unrecognized. Incarceration leads to a number of issues which can negatively impact family systems and exacerbate existing problems. Poverty, substandard housing, food insecurity, lack of sufficient medical care, and past child abuse and/or neglect are among the risk factors that may have an increased impact on children if a parent is in prison or jail (Family, 2005). In one study of caregivers who brought children to visit a parent in prison, researchers found caregivers reported incarceration caused family problems, impacted families' financial stability, and led to declines in caregivers' health (Arditti, Lambert-Shute, & Joest, 2003).

Overall, there is little research available regarding how children are impacted and how they cope with parental incarceration, although there is data available on the impact of parental loss on children (Travis, Cincotta, & Solomon, 2005). Ann Adalist-Estrin has identified eight feelings that children report when coping with the incarceration of their primary caregiver: anger, confusion, fear, guilt, worry, sadness, loyalty conflict, and embarrassment (2002). It is important that these children are encouraged to express these feelings in healthy ways. Often children express themselves by withdrawing emotionally, or acting out through aggression, excessive risk taking, and/or rejection of authority (Adalist-Estrin, 2002). The impact of parental loss due to incarceration varies based on the child's age and developmental stage, and whether or not the parent was the primary caregiver prior to incarceration (Travis, Cincotta, & Solomon, 2005).

St. Louis City has the third highest incarceration rate in the state of Missouri (Department of Corrections, 2009). Given the prevalence of incarceration and the risks these families face as a result, it is important that community organizations take an active role in supporting children of incarcerated parents. There are a number of protective factors that help children mediate these risks. One of these has been identified as positive relationships with their extended family and other informal social networks (Family, 2005). Support groups which work to help children expand their social network and coping skills are one way to encourage positive relationships.

NOTE: Additional resources for information on incarceration and its impact on families are available in Appendix C on page 114.

References

Adalist-Estrin, A. "Homecoming: Children's Adjustment to Parent's Parole." In *Family & Corrections Network* (2002). http://www.billygrahamcenter.com/prisonministries/assets/files/adalist-es.pdf (accessed May 1, 2009).

Arditti, J.A., J. Lambert-Shute, and K. Joest. "Saturday Morning at the Jail: Implications of Incarceration for Families and Children." In *Family Relations* (2003): 52(3), 195–204.

Department of Corrections. "A Profile of the Institutional and Supervised Offender Population on June 20, 2008" (2009). http://www.doc.mo.gov/pdf/OffenderProfileFY08.pdf (accessed May 1, 2009).

Family Strengthening Policy Center. "Supporting Families with Incarcerated Parents" (2005). http://www.nydic.org/fspc/practice/documents/Brief8.pdf (accessed May 1, 2009).

Glaze, L, and L. Maruschak. "Parents in Prison and Their Minor Children." In *Bureau of Justice Statistics Special Report*, (2009). http://www.nydic.org/fspc/practice/documents/Brief8.pdf (accessed May 1, 2009).

Sabol, W., and H. Couture. "Prison Inmates at Midyear 2007." In *Bureau of Justice Statistics* (2008). http://www.ojp.usdoj.gov/bjs/pub/pdf/pim07.pdf (accessed May 1, 2009).

Travis, J., E. Cincotta, and A. Solomon. "Families Left Behind: The Hidden Costs of Incarceration and Reentry." Washington, D.C.: Urban Institute, 2005.

Let's Start with the Kids

✓ Goals and Objectives

Goal 1

To facilitate peer support amongst children of incarcerated parents, focusing on building healthy relationships and safety in the group.

Objectives:

A welcoming, fun, and safe atmosphere will be cultivated by setting clear group guidelines and encouraging all children to participate.

Adults who have had a parent who was incarcerated during their childhood will serve as co-facilitators with professional staff. These co-facilitators will serve as role models for student participants.

Each student will have the option of being included on a student contact phone list in order to facilitate connections and support between group members.

Students and their families will have access to information about community resources and referrals from Let's Start or the school social worker.

Outcomes:

Students will self-report feelings supported by the group as measured by a post-group evaluation survey.

Students will self-report that co-facilitators acted as positive role models as measured by a post-group evaluation survey.

A phone list will be distributed to all participating students.

All students and caregivers who request or are identified by staff as potentially benefiting from additional resources will receive a follow-up administered by Let's Start staff and/or the school social worker.

Goal 2

Children will be able to identify and articulate their feelings regarding the incarceration of their parent and will have the opportunity to practice coping skills for negative feelings.

Objectives:

Group activities will include discussion of children's feelings about the incarceration of their parent and role-playing healthy coping strategies.

Co-facilitators will share how they felt and coped with their feelings while their parents were in prison or jail.

Outcomes:

80 percent of participants will report knowledge of coping skills for dealing with sadness, shame, guilt, and anger as measured by a post-group evaluation survey.

60 percent will report using healthy coping methods discussed in the group as measured by a post-group evaluation survey.

60 percent of caregivers and teachers/school social workers will report observing children's improved coping skills as measured by pre- and post-group evaluation surveys.

Goal 3

Children will learn and practice healthy decision-making skills.

Objectives:

Group activities will include discussion of strategies for making healthy choices and taking responsibility for one's actions.

Outcomes:

60 percent of participants will self-report making better decisions since beginning the group as measured by pre- and post-test evaluation surveys.

60 percent of caregivers will report that children make better decisions since attending the group as measured by pre- and post-test evaluation surveys.

School social worker will report that 60 percent of children make healthier decisions since attending the group as measured by pre- and post-test evaluation surveys.

✓ Implementation Process (2009–2010)

A social worker in the University City School District (UCSD) invited Let's Start to a discussion about the impact of parental incarceration on children. In her relationships with students, she was becoming increasingly aware that there were numerous children in the UCSD schools who had a parent in jail or prison. She was also aware that early interventions in the lives of these children were essential. Let's Start offered to provide a pilot support group process for the district at a school of their choosing. In collaboration with UCSD, the following process took place:

1. A meeting was held with all the social workers in the district and with Let's Start representatives.

2. Let's Start representatives made a presentation to the School Board addressing the specific challenges these children face and offered to provide a support group for them.

3. After the School Board approved the group process, planning was begun to implement a fourth-grade group at a district elementary school.

4. A survey was distributed to all the children in grade four to determine their eligibility for group participation. Only children who currently had a parent in prison or jail were included in the pilot group.

5. The school social worker obtained written permission from the students' caregivers for their participation in the group sessions.

6. Groups began in the spring and were conducted for ten weeks.

Let's Start developed the curriculum, using research and building on its years of experience in working with children who have an incarcerated parent. Let's Start also put together a facilitation team that included an educator, a Master's level social work practicum student, and two young adults who had an incarcerated parent while growing up. The young adults' presence was invaluable because they could share their experiences and be positive role models for the children. The school social worker was also an integral part of each session. She was present for each session and was available to conduct follow-up meetings with students as needed throughout the process.

The key elements of each session were as follows:

1. The children came with their lunch (since the group session was held during their lunch period) and spent a few minutes in informal group time to settle in each week.

2. Every group began with a review of the group rules, which was done verbally and using visual prompts. The following rules were agreed upon in the first session:

    a. Keep your eyes on the person talking.

    b. Use a listening ear. Don't talk while others are sharing.

    c. Care about each other. Never laugh or make fun of someone.

    d. Personal information shared in the group must not be shared outside the group.

3. Following the curriculum, each session had a theme and accompanying activities. All the facilitators present were included in the discussions and activities with the children.

4. All sessions ended with a period in which the children wrote in their journals. At the end of the year they were able to keep their journals.

5. With their permission, a contact list was compiled so that the students had a way to stay in contact after the group process concluded.

✓ Curriculum

SESSION 1: Getting to Know One Another

Focus:

• The students and facilitators introduce themselves.

• Students and facilitators begin to foster trust and safety, and encourage sharing.

Tasks:

1. Review group rules.

2. Sharing: Introductions

   Questions for discussion:

   • What is your name & who takes care of you?
     Example: My name is _____. I'm in fourth grade and I live with my grandmother because my dad/mom is in prison.

   • What is something I enjoy doing when I'm not in school?

   • What is something I enjoy doing when I'm at school?

   • What is something I like about the person who takes care of me?

   • What is something my caregiver likes about me?

   One of the facilitators is invited to respond first to model responses for the students. Each student is asked to respond to each question.

3. Group Activity:

Students are divided into two groups. Each group is given a worksheet with the names of the people in the other group. Next to each name they list something positive about that person. A facilitator is a part of each group. After a few minutes, individual students are called, they stand, and the group tells them some positive qualities they see in them.

Example:

Student 1 – He's outgoing; smart; likes to have fun

Student 2 – She's generous; nice looking; truthful

Student 3 – She has a good personality; you can trust her

Facilitator – She cares about other people; she is hard working

4. Student Self Evaluation Form *(See Appendix B)*:

With their mentor, students respond to the requested information. They are encouraged to talk about each statement as they write their written responses.

5. Journaling:

Each person in the group receives a journal. They are asked to write their name on the cover. Each session includes time for journal writing on a specific topic. Every week the journals are collected by the facilitators at the end of the session, and students are assured that no one will read them.

SESSION 2:
Understanding Feelings –
Happiness and Sadness

Focus:

• Students identify feelings of sadness and happiness and brainstorm ideas for coping with sadness.

Tasks:

1. Review group rules.

2. Sharing:

   Each participant completes the following sentences:

   • One thing that makes me feel happy is _____.

   • One thing that makes me feel sad is _____.

   The group brainstorms ideas about things they can do when they feel sad. They are encouraged to talk about what they actually do.

   Responses included such things as playing football, eating ice cream, talking to my friend, taking a nap, and writing in my journal. One of the facilitators shared that he listens to music when he is sad. Afterwards he planned to bring a music CD to the next group session for each of the students. This CD was used throughout later sessions.

3. Activity: *Comic strip*

   In groups of students and facilitators, students draw a comic strip that tells a story about one way of dealing with sadness. They share completed comics with one another *(See Appendix A)*.

4. Journaling:

Topic - Write about how you are feeling today.

5. Closing:

What was one thing you liked about today's group?

SESSION 3:
Understanding Feelings - Anger

Focus:

• Students identify circumstances when they feel angry and list ideas for coping with anger.

Tasks:

1. Review group rules.

2. Sharing:

> Students share a time when they felt angry. They are encouraged to tell about a time when they felt angry because their parent is in prison. (The facilitators who have had an incarcerated parent speak first to model sharing.) Students briefly share how they acted out their anger—they identify if their behavior was positive or negative.

3. Brainstorming:

> Students brainstorm positive ways to deal with anger. Ideas are recorded on the board. Each student then goes to the paper, points to and reads one idea that they think helps them act in a positive way when they are angry.

> As follow up to this activity the list of ideas brainstormed in group was put together on a bookmark and distributed to students the following week. *(See Appendix A)*

4. Journaling:

> Topic - Write about a time when you were angry and about positive ways to deal with that anger. The CD is played as background music.

SESSION 4:
Building Relationships - Trust

Focus:

• Students discuss the concept of "trust" and identify people who can be trusted with the truth about having a parent in prison or jail.

Tasks:

1. Review group rules.

2. Sharing: *Identifying people we trust*

   Part 1: Students name a person whom they trust and why they trust that person.

   Part 2: Co-facilitators who experienced parental incarceration tell a story about how they shared their feelings about their parent in prison with someone they could trust. Each student is invited to name a person they feel they could trust to tell that their dad is in prison. In some cases there may be no one whom they trust enough.

   Part 3: Students are assured that everyone in this room are people they can trust. Students are asked to share with us what they would like to say to or about their dad. They can pass if they choose.

3. Activity:

   A story is read about a child with a father in prison. This story is printed as a handout for each student. *(See Appendix A)* Students are invited to take turns reading this out loud and afterwards each student is asked to share one thought or feeling about the story.

4. Journaling:

Topic - Describe your feelings about the story in their journals. The CD is played as background music.

SESSION 5:
Sharing Our Stories, Part I

Focus:

• A co-facilitator who has experienced the incarceration of her or his parent will share their story with the group.

• Students are encouraged to share their own story.

Tasks:

1. Review group rules.

2. Sharing:

Part 1: The facilitator reads her or his story regarding the incarceration of a parent *(See Appendix A)*. Students are invited to respond to the story by sharing with the facilitator any thoughts or feelings they might have.

Part 2: Students are given paper (or they can use their journals) so they can write and/or draw about their own experiences and feelings about having a parent in prison. They are then invited to share their story.

3. Mid-group evaluation:

Each person will name one thing they like about the group

One of the facilitators' group goals was to include the children's caregivers in the process by providing information and support to them when possible. Connecting with parents/caregivers was a challenge.

During week six, parent/teacher conferences were held at the school. The facilitators made themselves available for a designated period of time to meet with the caregivers of the student participants. A caregiver resource guide and a caregiver evaluation form were available for each family and were later distributed via surface mail.

SESSION 6:
Celebrating Achievements –
Pizza Party!

Focus:

• Students are invited to name and claim the accomplishments they have made in group up to this point.

Tasks:

1. Pizza party with informal sharing

2. Journaling

SESSION 7:
Sharing Our Stories, Part II

Focus:

• A co-facilitator who has experienced the incarceration of her or his parent shares his/her story with the group.

• Students are encouraged to share their own story.

Tasks:

1. Review group rules.

2. Sharing:

> *Part 1*: The facilitator reads her or his story regarding the incarceration of her/his parent.

> *Part 2*: Children are given a worksheet with follow-up questions to the story *(See Appendix A)*. After a few minutes of quiet writing time, the facilitator reads each question and students respond.

> Different types of activities—reading, writing, and speaking activities—were used throughout the group in order to encourage various forms of expression, and as a way to keep kids engaged in the process. Quiet writing activities were used especially when kids were having difficulty focusing or when they seemed to be dealing with intense emotional issues.

3. Activity: *Friendship Advertisement*

The facilitator's story focused on the ability to share one's experience with friends and a caring adult. Children are reminded that a good friend can often help us deal with our feelings. Students will draw an advertisement for a good friend and share what qualities they look for in a friend *(See Appendix A)*. Sample ads are displayed and discussed in order to stimulate brainstorming.

SESSION 8:
Healthy Decision Making

Focus:

• Students talk about making healthy choices and taking responsibility for consequences of decisions.

Tasks:

1. Review group rules.

2. Sharing: *"What if . . . ?"*

> Facilitator reads the following prepared statements and students write down what choices they might make and the consequences of those choices on the "Choices & Consequences" worksheet *(See Appendix A).* As a group students share their answers.

Possible situations:

> a. You are on the playground with some of your friends. One of them hits you.

> b. You are in the grocery store and you really want some candy but you do not have enough money to pay for it.

> c. You are having an important test in school. There are some questions that you do not know the answer for. You can see the answers on the paper of the person across from you.

> d. Your dad wants you to come visit him in prison but you do not like going to the prison.

> e. Your friends realize that they never see you with your dad and want to know why he is never with you.

> f. You see your friend crying because she is sad. When you ask her why she is sad, she says she misses her dad who is in prison.

3. Journaling:

Topic - What am I feeling today? The CD is played as background music.

SESSION 9:
Providing Support

Focus:

• Students develop skills in supporting peers and the practice of positive self talk.

Tasks:

1. Review group rules.

2. Sharing:

> The facilitator reads vignettes below, and students record how they would respond to the person in each vignette: Students can write their responses before sharing *(See Appendix A)*.

> a. Daniel told his counselor, "I don't like this school. None of the kids want to play with me." What would you say to Daniel?

> b. David is teased at school because his parents are never with him. He always thinks, "My mom and dad are in prison. Maybe if I lie and say they are working in another state, the kids will stop teasing me." What would you say to David?

> c. Emily thought to herself, "I'm mad at my dad. He's in prison and I never want to see him again." What would you say to Emily?

> d. Mary thinks to herself, "I'm not going to play with the other kids because they know my dad uses crack and they will make fun of me." What would you say to Mary?

> e. Jean thinks, "I just know it is my fault that my dad is in prison." What would you say to Jean?

> f. Marsha is in the hall at school crying. When asked why she is crying, she says, "I'm crying because my dad is going to prison." What would you say to Marsha?

g. Susan is sitting in the corner thinking, "I'm so scarred. My dad is coming home from prison and I don't know what to do or say." What would you say to Susan?

3. Activity:

Each student is given a paper (or they can use their journal) on which they are to write a statement about a situation, a feeling, or a concern they are experiencing or may experience in the future. Students will share their statements with the group.

Example:

I am _____

What would I say to myself?_____

4. Closing:

Students are reminded that next week is the last week of group. They are asked for permission to be included on a telephone list of everyone in the group so students and facilitators can continue to support each other.

SESSION 10:
Closing and Evaluation

Focus:

• Students participate in a final evaluation of the group process.

Tasks:

1. Review group rules.

2. Sharing:

> Students fill out a questionnaire regarding the group experience (Student Group Evaluation Form, p. 44). Students then share their responses to the following questions with the group.

> Sample evaluation questions for discussion:
> • What did you like about the group?
>
> • What are you feeling right now?
>
> • What would you like to say to yourself about how you are feeling?
>
> • What is one way you can deal with feelings of anger?
>
> • Right now, what are you feeling about your parent who is in prison?
>
> • What do you want to say to yourself about those feelings?
>
> • Since these group sessions have begun, do you feel more comfortable and more able to talk about your feelings?

3. Closing:

Facilitators express their gratitude to the students for allowing them to be a part of their lives. A phone contact list is distributed and the journals were given to the students so they can continue journaling.

✓ Moving Forward

Insights and Reflections

Over the years, Let's Start has become increasingly aware that children are radically impacted by parental incarceration. Thus, we have committed ourselves to providing various types of support for these children. The group process offered at an elementary school in University City was one such effort. We believe this process was beneficial to the students who participated. They received peer support, interacted with positive role models, grew in their ability to articulate their feelings, and learned various methods of coping with feelings and making positive choices. Below are some insights and lessons we gained from this experience. As we continue to offer group sessions, we will continue to reflect on our experience and make adjustments to improve the process.

1. *Scheduling such sessions in an academic day can be challenging.* Group sessions were scheduled during the students' lunch period and recess time; yet attendance was perfect (except when the students missed school because of illness). We believe the children not only learned something from the group process, but they also sincerely enjoyed it.

2. *It takes time to develop trust.* As we reflect back on the process, it was in session five that the students began to talk freely about their feelings regarding their incarcerated fathers.

3. *Having two young adults who had an incarcerated parent while they were growing up provided excellent role models for the children.* The students seemed to be inspired by them, and they provided "hope" for the children.

4. *Stories about children who also had experienced the incarceration of a parent encouraged the students to talk more openly about their personal stories.* These stories provided a backdrop and modeling for them to share and reflect on their experiences.

5. *The presence of the school social worker at each session was invaluable.* She knew the students prior to the start of the group and provided them with a known level of comfort. She was also available to follow up with any student who needed additional support. After session six, one of the students requested a personal session with her.

6. *Evaluation.* As we began this process, our goal was to use a standardized evaluation to measure our outcomes. We researched self-esteem and behavioral evaluations. We decided to use the self-esteem evaluation; however, we came to realize that it did not adequately measure the program's goals. Therefore, as we moved forward, we created our own evaluation form geared specifically to our goals and objectives. *Appendix B* contains sample evaluation tools.

7. *Contact and communication with the parent or caregiver was deemed important, but was difficult to achieve.* We made ourselves available during parent-teacher conferences but were not successful in meeting any of the caregivers. Therefore, a resource guide was mailed to each of them during week six. Prior to the start of the group process, the school social worker contacted caregivers, obtaining their permission for children to participate in the program.

Kent Nerburn once said, "A sailor lost at sea can be guided home by a single candle. A person lost in a wood can be led to safety by a flickering flame. It is not an issue of quality or intensity or purity. It is simply an issue of the presence of light." It is the goal of *Let's Start with the Kids* to provide that "flicker of light" to the children engaged in these support groups.

Appendix A
In-Group Handouts

SESSION 2:
Feelings Comic Strip Handout

Feelings Comic Strip

Title:

Name:

SESSION 3:
Bookmark

Create a bookmark on POSITIVE WAYS OF COPING WITH ANGER
(ideas are generated by the students)

- Writing
- Drawing
- Prayer
- Riding a bike
- Taking a walk
- Listening to music
- Going shopping
- Dancing!
- Spending time in my room
- Going to the movies
- Going to Grandpa's
- Eating ice cream or my favorite food
- Skating
- Playing a game
- Playing with dolls
- Playing Nintendo, Wii, or PSP
- Calling a cousin, a relative, or someone close to me

SESSION 4:
Creating "Feeling" Stories

Story of a Child with a Father in Prison

My dad doesn't live with me right now. My dad made some bad decisions and now he lives in prison. I hate it when people ask me where my dad is. I'm always afraid people will make fun of me. Or maybe they won't want to be my friend if I tell them where my dad lives.

I like to get letters or cards from my dad. It makes my day very special. Dad tells me he loves me and thinks of me. I believe him.

I also get a little sad when I get a letter or card from my dad. Other kids don't have to get letters from their dad. Other kids get to live in the same house with their dad and do things with him.

I really wish I could spend some time with my dad. Sometimes I am very mad at my dad for being in prison. My mom says it's okay for me to be mad at my dad. She tells me to find people I trust and tell them how I feel. That will help me, she says.

I really, really wish my dad lived in the same house with me. I believe he would like to be home with me too. I have a nice family and some friends who take care of me and do things with me. But no one else can take the place of my dad.

SESSION 5:
Creating Stories of Meaning by Mentor Witnessing

J's Story

My name is J and this is my story. I was only five when my mom went to prison. I remember my granny telling me my mom lost her job and then one day she told me she was in jail. At first I felt kinda sad and then I got over it. I was okay when my granny told me she was coming home sometime. I stayed at my granny's house. The hardest thing was that I couldn't talk on the phone very long because the phone would cut off and I didn't have a chance to say bye to my mom.

One time I visited her. It was Christmas. They had gifts. They let us play games and take pictures. I game my mom a big hug and I kissed her. That was the best part—kissing my mom. After we left, I was mad because it was the only time I could see her till she came home.

For a while I stayed at my granny's house. Then my godmother took us away from my grandmother. She didn't take us like she was mean—she just took us. And we stayed with her. I didn't tell my friends where my mom was. I'd say, "My mother, she's just gone away." I just told one boy and he didn't tell anybody. I trusted him.

I was nine when she came home. I was so happy to see her and she was happy to see me. Now things are good. I am in college and I want to be a teacher so I can help other children.

SESSION 7:
Creating Stories of Meaning by Mentor Witnessing:

R's Story

This is my story. My name is R but my friends call me Ro. My father was out of work a lot. But one day he got a job as a dog catcher. He was a quiet man but he had a violent temper. One day at work he got into a serious fight. Then my mother left him. The police were looking for him so he took me with him. One day he went to jail. I did not know what jail was at that time, but I already knew that people in my family were not there for me. Eventually, my father came home from jail.

For a while I lived with my grandmother, but she was getting too old to take care of me. My mother was in prison too. She used drugs and she stole things. So I was sent to live with my father and my stepmother. My father would hit me and beat me a lot. So I acted out in school. I got bad grades and sometimes got into fights. One day I went to school with black eyes. The social worker helped me by taking me to the emergency room. Then I was placed in a foster home.

My foster parents were good to me. My mother would send me letters from prison, but I didn't want them. I was mad at her too. Because both of my parents were in prison, I though I would go there too. But when I was in junior high, I met some nice people. I started visiting my mom in prison. My mother told me she would be out of prison by the time I graduated from high school. My mother kept her word and was out of prison to see me in a few track meets and to see me graduate.

I went to college to major in graphic design. Now I am studying to be an engineer. I live with my mother and we are good friends now. What I learned is that I never want to see or go to a prison again. With the help of many friends who support me and with the help of my teachers, I know I will be strong and will never go to prison. I hope other children who have a parent in prison will be strong too.

SESSION 7 cont'd.: R's STORY – WORKSHEET on FEELINGS and COPING SKILLS

1. After you heard R's story, how did you feel? (write one word)

2. What do you think was the hardest thing for R? Why?

3. R says he met some nice people who helped him? Who are some nice people who are helping you? How are they helping?

4. Pretend you are R's best friend. After hearing his story, what would you tell him?

5. When you feel sad, what is one thing you can do to make yourself feel better?

6. When you feel mad or angry, what is one positive thing you can do to make yourself feel better?

SESSION 7: WANTED: a good friend

(students draw an advertisement)

SESSION 8: Naming/Understanding CHOICES and Their CONSEQUENCES

RESPONSE SHEET – CHOICES & CONSEQUENCES

For each situation write a choice that could be made and the consequences of each choice.

CHOICE	CONSEQUENCE
1.	
2.	
3.	
4.	
5.	
6.	

SESSION 9:
IMAGINING WHAT IF: What Would You Say To _____?

1. Daniel?

2. David?

3. Emily?

4. Mary?

5. Jean?

6. Marsha?

7. Susan?

I am concerned about (describe the situation):

What would I say to myself?

Appendix B
Sample Forms and Surveys

SAMPLE LETTER TO PARENTS/CAREGIVERS

To parents / caregivers of children with incarcerated parent(s)

Dear _____:

As you know, there are many children in our community who are being raised by someone other than their parents. This happens for many reasons: addiction, incarceration, divorce, etc. These children in our schools are facing unique challenges because of parental separation. Your school is starting a special group process for these children—children who have a parent inside the criminal justice system. Let's Start, a support process for women and their children, will facilitate these sessions for designated students starting ___(date)___. We would like to invite _(child's name)_ to be part of this group.

Over the course of 10 weeks, Let's Start will provide facilitators to assist students in dealing with separation issues due to parental incarceration. They will discuss issues related to self esteem, trust, anger, and choices and consequences. They will also focus on helping students identify their strengths and talents. The goal is to help each student develop coping skills and improve their behavior in school and at home.

If you are willing to have _____(student name)_____ participate in these group sessions, please complete the enclosed forms and return them to the school social worker.

We look forward to working with you.
Sincerely,

Let's Start
1408 S. 10th St.
St. Louis, MO 63104

Caregiver Permission Form

I, _____ hereby
give my permission for _____
to participate in the *Let's Start with the Kids* group process held at
_____(school name)_____.

    I hereby give permission for the group facilitators to allow school teachers, counselors, and social workers to respond to evaluations concerning my child's behavior before and after the group process, in order to help evaluate the effectiveness of this support group.

    I understand that I, as the caregiver of this student, will be invited to participate in specific group sessions and activities designed to support me in my role as caregiver.

    I understand that I can schedule an appointment with the school counselor or social worker or the Let's Start facilitators at any time to discuss my child's needs and concerns.

NAME: _____

ADDRESS: _____

PHONE: _____

SIGNATURE: _____

Caregiver Information Form

NAME: _____

ADDRESS: _____

ZIP CODE: _____

PHONE: _____

EMAIL: _____

Name of child who will participate in the *Let's Start with the Kids* group:

_____

Child's Age: _____

1. What are the strengths, talents, and/or gifts of this child?

2. On a scale of 1 to 10 with 10 being the most challenging, how would you rate the behavior of the child right now? _____

3. What specific behavior challenges is this child having (e.g., missing or skipping school, being disrespectful, acting out in class, fighting, etc.)? Please include behavior both at home and at school.

4. How often does the child have contact with the parent who is incarcerated? *Please check the best answer.*

❑ 2-3 times a week   ❑ Every few months
❑ Once a week   ❑ Only when the parent is not in prison/jail
❑ Once a month   ❑ Never

5. What kind of contact does the child have with the parent in prison/jail?

❑ Phone calls   ❑ Letters
❑ Visits   ❑ No contact

6. Does the child have close friends?

YES   NO

7. Does the child have difficulty coping with her/his feelings?

YES   NO

8. Does the child have a difficult time making good decisions?

YES   NO

9. Would you like to receive information about other programs available for children with a parent in prison or jail?

YES   NO

10. Do you have any other concerns about this child which are not being addressed?

Student Participation Eligibility Survey

NAME: _____

1. Do you have a parent who is in prison or jail now?

      YES   NO

2. Which parent is in prison/jail?

      MOTHER   FATHER   BOTH

3. How long has your parent been in prison/jail?

      ❏ 3 months   ❏ 6 months
      ❏ 1 year or longer   ❏ I don't know

4. Do you visit your parent in prison/jail?

      YES   NO

5. Do you write letters to your parent or talk to them on the phone while they are in prison?

      YES   NO

6. Do you have a parent that has been in prison but is not in prison anymore?

      YES   NO   Who?   MOTHER   FATHER

SAMPLE PARENT/CAREGIVER EVALUATION FORM

Support Group Parent/Caregiver Evaluation

NAME: _____

Name of child who attended the support group: _____

Please circle or write the answer to the questions below.

1. Overall has participation in the support group been beneficial for your child or grandchild? Please circle your answer.

      YES   NO   I DON'T KNOW

   1a. Why or why not?

2. On a scale of 1 to 10 with 10 being the most challenging, how would you rate the behavior of the child who attended the group? _____

3. Have you noticed a change in your child or grandchild's behavior since he or she began the group?

YES   NO   I DON'T KNOW

3a. If you answered yes to question 3, please check all of the following that apply:

Has your child:
❑ Talked more about having a parent in prison/jail
❑ Communicated with the incarcerated parent
❑ Used healthy coping skills in a stressful situation
❑ Talked about her or his feelings
❑ Made better decision
❑ Other (Please be specific)

4. How often does the child have contact with the incarcerated parent? Please check the best answer:

❑ 2-3 times a week   ❑ Every few months
❑ Once a week   ❑ Only when the parent is not in prison/jail
❑ Once a month   ❑ Never

5. What kind of contact does the child have with the parent in prison/jail?

❑ Phone calls   ❑ Letters
❑ Visits   ❑ Other
❑ No contact

6. While your child was participating in the support group did you receive information about any resources or other organizations that might be helpful to your family?

YES   NO

7. Would you recommend this group for other children with a parent in prison or jail?

YES   NO   I DON'T KNOW

7a. Why or why not?

8. Are there any other needs related to parental incarceration you think your child has that are not being addressed?

Additional Comments:
Please share any additional comments you have about the group process and your child's participation in the group.

Student Group Evaluation

1. What did you enjoy about the support group?

2. Did you feel supported from the others in the group?

     YES   NO

3. What is one positive thing you can do when you feel:

- Angry?

- Sad?

- Shame?

4. What is a coping skill you used during the last month to deal with your anger or sadness?

5. What is a good behavioral decision you made during the last month?

6. What was the most helpful thing about the group?

7. How do you feel right now about your parent who is in prison/jail?

      If a friend told you he or she was feeling that way, what would you say to them?

8. Name one new thing that you learned from attending the group.

9. Did the facilitators act as positive role models for you?

     YES   NO

10. What is one thing you would change about the group?

Intake and Evaluation Form
(Students)

STUDENT NAME: _____

DATE: _____

Please circle the most applicable answer below.

Rating Scale:

1	2	3	4	5	6
Excellent			Average		Needs Improvement

1. I follow directions in class.   _____

2. I listen to my teacher in class.   _____

3. I turn in my homework on time.   _____

4. I raise my hand to speak in class.   _____

5. I come to school every day.   _____

6. I talk politely to other students.   _____

Please write a short response to the following statements:

1. Write the name of one good friend that you can trust.

_____

2. Write one positive action you can do when you feel angry.

_____

3. Write one thing you can do when you feel sad.

_____

Comments:

Intake and Evaluation Form
(Teachers/Social Workers/Counselors)

STUDENT NAME: _____

DATE: _____

TEACHER/SOCIAL WORKER: _____

Please circle the most applicable answer below.

Rating Scale:

1	2	3	4	5	6
Excellent		Average		Needs Improvement	

1. He/she follows directions in class. _____

2. He/she listens to the teacher in class. _____

3. He/she turns in my homework on time. _____

4. He/she raises his/her hand to speak in class. _____

5. He/she comes to school every day. _____

6. He/she talks politely to other students. _____

Please write a short response to the following statements:

1. Can you name one good friend that this student has? Explain.

_____

2. Does this child respond in a positive way to feelings of anger? Explain.

_____

3. Does this child respond in a positive way to feelings of sadness? Explain.

_____

Comments:

Let's Start with the Kids

Year 2

Contents

Introduction

Let's Start is an organization led by and for formerly incarcerated women which aims to break the cycle of incarceration in families *by using the personal experiences of its participants to support individual recovery, educate the community, and inform public policy*.

Over the past years, Let's Start has become more and more aware that children are profoundly impacted by the incarceration of a parent. Thus, we have begun to implement various support systems for families. One such support is the group process begun in 2009 for fourth graders at an elementary school in University City, Missouri. A decision was made to continue the group sessions with these same children. This decision was made at the request of the children and with the recommendation of the school social worker. Thus, the group continued.

Research has shown that children of prisoners have numerous material needs. Beyond that, however, other less tangible, but equally compelling needs are present. In a publication titled "Children of Incarcerated Parents: A Bill of Rights," published by the San Francisco Partnership for Incarcerated Children, these needs are clearly expressed: "They (the children) need to be told the truth about their parents' situation. They need someone to listen without judging, so that their parents' status need not remain a secret. They need the companionship of others who share their experience, so they can know they are not alone. They need contact with their parents to have that relationship recognized and valued even under adverse circumstances. And, rather than being stigmatized for their parent's actions or status, they need to be treated with respect, offered opportunity, and recognized as having potential."

Building on the goals, objectives, and activities of Year One, the curriculum for Year Two was developed. The group rules used during the previous year were continued. The young adults who grew up with a parent in prison were available at each session to assist with the facilitation and to act as positive role models for the students. Permission to participate in these sessions was obtained from the caregiver of each child. The sessions were held during the lunch and recess period, so each session began with informal time as the children ate their lunch. The school social worker was present for each session and was able to schedule individual sessions with the children as needed or as requested. The entire time with the students was 50 minutes.

Let's Start with the Kids

✓ Goals and Objectives

Goal 1

To facilitate peer support amongst children of incarcerated parents, focusing on building healthy relationships and safety in the group.

Objectives:

A welcoming, fun, and safe atmosphere will be cultivated by setting clear group guidelines and encouraging all children to participate.

Adults who have had a parent who was incarcerated during their childhood will serve as co-facilitators with professional staff. These co-facilitators will serves as role models for student participants.

Each student will have the option of being included on a student contact phone list in order to facilitate connections and support between group members.

Students and their families will have access to information about community resources and referrals from Let's Start or the school social worker.

Outcomes:

Students will-self report feeling supported by the group as measured by a pre- and post-group evaluation survey.

Students will self-report that co-facilitators acted as positive role models as measured by a post-group evaluation survey.

A phone list will be distributed to all participating students.

All students and caregivers who request or are identified by staff as potentially benefiting from additional resources will receive a follow-up administered by Let's Start staff and/or the school social worker.

Goal 2

Children will be able to identify and articulate their feelings regarding the incarceration of their parent and will have the opportunity to identify coping skills for negative feelings.

Objectives:

Group activities will include discussion of children's feelings about the incarceration of their parent, and healthy coping strategies will be discussed.

Co-facilitators will share how they felt and coped with their feelings while their parents were in prison or jail.

Outcomes:

80 percent of participants will report knowledge of coping skills for dealing with sadness, shame, guilt, and anger as measured by a post-group evaluation survey.

60 percent will report using healthy coping methods discussed in the group as measured by a post-group evaluation survey.

50 percent of caregivers and teachers/school social workers will report observing children's improved coping skills as measured by pre- and post-group evaluation surveys.

Goal 3

Children will learn and practice healthy decision-making skills.

Objectives:

Group activities will include discussion of strategies for making healthy choices and taking responsibility for one's actions.

Outcomes:

60 percent of participants will self-report making better decisions since beginning the group as measured by pre- and post-test evaluation surveys.

60 percent of caregivers will report that children make better decisions since attending the group as measured by pre- and post-test evaluation surveys.

School social worker will report that 60 percent of children make healthier decisions since attending the group as measured by pre- and post-test evaluation surveys.

Goal 4

Students will engage in activities that foster confidence and competence.

Objectives:

Group activities will include writing activities that allow students to creatively express some of the concepts previously discussed and what they have learned about confronting some of the challenges they face.

Students will engage in some public speaking activities.

Outcomes:

100 percent of the students will contribute writing and/or art samples to a booklet to be shared with others.

100 percent of the students will speak at a book-signing event sponsored by the group.

✓ Implementation Process (2009-2010)

A social worker in the University City School District (UCSD) invited Let's Start to continue the group process with the same students who had participated in 2008–09. In her interactions with the students, they were requesting that their group continue. Let's Start agreed to this arrangement.

The key elements of each session for Year Two were as follows:

1. The children came with their lunch (since the group session was held during their lunch period) and spent a few minutes in informal group time to settle in each week.

2. Every group began with a review of the group rules, which was done verbally and using visual prompts. The following rules were agreed upon in the first session:

   a. Keep your eyes on the person who is talking.

   b. Use a listening ear. Don't talk while others are talking.

   c. Care about each other. Never laugh or make fun of someone.

   d. Personal information shared in the group must not be shared outside the group. There was discussion about how the kids could explain to their caregivers that they did not have to talk about things they did not want to discuss.

3. Following the curriculum, each session had a theme and accompanying activities. All the facilitators present were included in the discussions and activities with the children.

4. Each session began with an activity focusing on what students were feeling right now. They were encouraged to talk briefly about that feeling in the context of what was happening in their lives.

5. Writing activities were frequently used after session four. At the conclusion of the sessions, their writing was compiled into a booklet. Some of their art work was also used. A book-signing event was scheduled toward the end of the process.

6. With their permission, a contact list was compiled so that students had a way to stay connected after the group process concluded.

✓ Curriculum

SESSION 1:
Getting to Know One Another

Focus:

• The students and facilitators introduce themselves.

• Students and facilitators begin to foster trust and safety and encourage open and honest sharing.

Tasks:

1. Review group rules. These are posted and each is read aloud by one of the students.

2. Sharing: Introductions

Since the students know each other, they each are paired with a facilitator. In groups of two, they use the "Introduction of Self" activity *(See Appendix A)*. When all have completed the activity sheet, each student and/or facilitator introduces his/her partner.

3. Group Activity:

Students remain with their mentor. Each is given the "Student Self Evaluation Form" *(See Appendix B)*. With their mentor they respond to the requested information. They are encouraged to talk about each item as they write their response.

4. Journaling:

Each person in the group receives a journal. They are asked to write on the following topics:

1. What are some ways I can show support to others in the group?

2. What are some ways others can support me?

The journals are collected by the facilitators at the end of the session and students are assured that no one will read them.

SESSION 2:
Identifying Feelings; Naming Feelings

Focus:

• Students identify feelings they are currently experiencing.

• Students will increase their vocabulary in order to better name their feelings.

• Students will be able to name their feelings regarding their incarcerated parent.

Tasks:

1. Review group rules.

2. Sharing:

> A "feeling tree" is placed on the table. Leaves are placed around the tree, each of which has a feeling word written on it. Students are invited to choose a leaf that expresses what they are feeling right now. As each student and facilitator in turn states out loud the word on the "feeling" leaf he/she has chosen, that leaf is placed on the tree. Each person is invited to explain the reason for choosing that particular leaf.

3. Activity—Naming their feelings about their incarcerated parents.

> Each of the three facilitators who have had a parent in prison reads their story about their feelings toward that parent (See Appendix A).
>
> After each story, the students either ask a question or make a comment about the story. Then each student is invited to share what he/she is feeling about their parent in prison.

4. Journaling

   Topic - Write about the following: Right now, what is it that I would like to tell my dad?

5. Closing

   What is one thing you liked about today's group?

SESSION 3:
Identifying Feelings; Naming Feelings

Focus:

• Students will be able to identify and name their feelings.

• Students will be able to identify feelings about their incarcerated parent.

Tasks:

1. Review group rules.

2. Sharing:

   Our "feeling tree" is placed on the table. All are silent for a few minutes to think about how they are feeling right now. Then, all choose one leaf that best describes that feeling. The facilitator then calls each person by name and asks him/her to put the leaf on the tree, to say the feeling, and to explain, comment, or share about that feeling.

3. Naming feelings about their incarcerated parent:

   In a basket are some papers with beginning statements. Each student picks out one of the papers. Then the facilitator invites each student to read the statement on his/her paper and complete the statement. The statements used are as follows:

   • One happy time I remember about my dad is:

   • One sad time I remember about my dad is:

   • I remember a time when I was angry with my dad. This is what happened:

- I remember telling _____ about my dad being in prison. This is what happened:

- One thing I want to remember about my dad is:

4. Activity:

Students are given a "Feeling Word Search Activity" to complete. The words all relate to identifying and naming feelings *(See Appendix A)*.

SESSION 4:
Making Connections Between Feelings and Behavior

Focus:

• Students will identify and name the feelings they are experiencing.

• Students will recognize the connection between feelings and negative behavior.

Tasks:

1. Review group rules

2. Sharing:

> *Part 1*: Our "feeling tree" is placed on the table. All are silent for a few minutes to think about what they are feeling right now. Then, all choose a leaf that best describes their feeling. The facilitator then calls each person by name and asks him/her to put their leaf on the tree, to say their feeling, and to explain, comment, or share about that feeling.

> *Part 2*: The facilitator explains to the group that our feelings sometimes influence our behavior. If I am sad, I may withdraw. If I am angry, I may talk back to my teacher. If I am excited, I may act out or forget to do my assignment. The facilitator then asks each student to think of one negative behavior that students see in their classroom. As each behavior is named, it is written on a piece of posted paper. The facilitator then explains to the student that if we want to change that negative behavior, we have to THINK BEFORE WE ACT. Then the

facilitator goes through each behavior written on the board and invites the students to share how that behavior could have been different if the person THINKS BEFORE HE/SHE ACTS.

Part 3: Students are given the worksheet: THINK BEFORE YOU ACT *(See Appendix A)*. On the bottom of the sheet they are to write a negative behavior. Then, in the circle, they are to write the behavior that would have happened if the person THINKS BEFORE HE/SHE ACTS. After all have completed the activity, each student stands before the group and reads the situation described on his/her paper.

3. Journaling

Topic - Students write in their journals about how they want to act at school, at home and with their friends.

SESSION 5:
Naming Feelings and Exhibiting Positive Behavior

Focus:

• Students will name what they are currently feeling.

• Students will engage in positive behavior as they complete the activity for the day.

Tasks:

1. Review group rules.

2. Sharing

> *Part 1, Naming feelings*: Our feeling tree is placed on the table. All are silent for a few minutes to think about what they are feeling right now. Then, all choose a leaf that best describes that feeling. The facilitator then calls each person by name and asks him/her to put their leaf on the tree, to say their feeling and to explain, comment or share about that feeling.

> *Part 2*: Since this session occurs immediately before the holiday break, the students are invited to draw cards for their incarcerated dad or for another family member. They could also simply draw as they feel.

3. Mid-group evaluation:

> Each person names one thing they like about the group.

SESSION 6, 7, 8: Writing about Feelings, Choices, and Behaviors

Focus:

• Students will name feelings they are currently experiencing.

• Students will write about those feelings, about decision making and about the importance of a healthy self-esteem.

Tasks:

1. During the next three weeks, students engage in writing activities with their mentor. At the beginning of each session, they continue to use the "feeling tree" to name and explain what they are currently feeling. Then they move to different sections of the room to write. A writing packet is given to each student so they can proceed with the writing at their own pace *(See Appendix A)*.

Towards the end of each session, every student chooses one thing they wrote and reads it orally to the group.

2. Final activity:

The group session concludes each week with each student reading a "scenario" *(See Appendix A)* and responding to the situation described by answering the following questions:

• In this situation, what is he/she feeling?

• In this situation, what would she/he say to herself? What would he say to his mom?

• What would Dr. King, Rosa Parks, or President Obama say to him/her?

SESSION 9, 10, 11, 12:
Relating to Others with an Incarcerated Parent

Focus:

• Students will name feelings and identify positive responses to those feelings.

• Students will show empathy and understanding toward others who have a parent in prison.

Tasks: Week 9

1. Review group rules.

2. The "feeling tree" is placed on the table and students choose a leaf to express their current feeling.

3. The movie *When the Bough Breaks* is used to allow the students to see the challenges and responses of other children who had a parent in prison.

4. Before we start the movie we have a discussion about the title of the movie to make sure the children know its significance. The title was chosen from the nursery rhyme: *Rock a bye baby in the tree top. When the wind blows the cradle will rock. When the bough breaks, the cradle will fall, and down will come baby, cradle and all.* The first half of the movie is shown.

Tasks: Week 10

1. Review group rules.

2. The "feeling tree" is placed on the table and students choose a leaf to express their current feeling.

3. This session provides an opportunity for the children to process the first half of the movie *When the Bough Breaks*. A white paper tablecloth is placed on four tables. With their mentor, the teams move from table to table at designated times to express in art the feelings generated from the movie. At each table, a different art activity is used. The children draw their response on the tablecloth. The four activities are:

- How did you feel while watching the movie? Draw a picture that expresses that feeling.

- Choose one of the children from the movie. Draw a card that you would like to send to them.

- One of the children in the movie says that he draws his anger. Draw a picture of what anger looks like to you.

- You are special and deserve to be happy. Draw a picture of what makes you happy.

Tasks: Week 11

1. Review group rules.

2. The "feeling tree" is placed on the table and students choose a leaf to express their current feeling.

3. The final part of the movie is shown.

SESSION 12:
Relating to Others with an Incarcerated Parent

Focus:

• Students will name feelings and identify positive responses to those feelings.

• Students will show empathy and understanding toward others who have a parent in prison.

Tasks:

1. Review group rules.

2. The "feeling tree" is placed on the table and students choose a leaf to express their current feeling.

3. This session is used to process the second half of the movie *When the Bough Breaks*. Students are each given a paper copy of a school bus and are asked to imagine that they and their mentor are riding the bus to the prison just as the children in the movie did. Then they move from table to table (imagining they are riding the bus) to complete an activity at each table. The activities are:

  • Draw a picture that you want to give to your parent that expresses how you are feeling now.

  • Imagine you are sitting next to someone who rode the bus in the movie. What would you like to talk about with them? Write that conversation.

• Draw a picture that expresses a feeling you think one of the children on the bus felt. Put the name of that child on the picture.

• Draw a picture of something you saw on the bus trip that expresses a happy feeling.

SESSION 13:
Evaluation

Focus:

• Students will name feelings and identify positive responses to those feelings.

• Students will identify their feelings regarding the group process and name new learnings.

• Students will identify behavior changes they have realized.

Tasks:

1. Review group rules.

2. The "feeling tree" is placed on the table and students choose a leaf to express their current feeling.

3. The group becomes a "focus group" for the evaluation process. The facilitator has the students respond to the following questions:

   a. What is your favorite thing about coming to group?

   b. What is your least favorite thing about coming to group?

   c. Tell me about working with your partner—what was it like?

   d. Rate the group activities. What is your favorite activity/least favorite activity out of what we have done?

   e. Tell me two things you learned during group.

   f. Since coming to group, has your behavior in the classroom changed?

g. Before coming to group, did you ever talk to anyone about your dad in prison? How has it been since you've been able to talk about it?

h. What is a piece of advice you would give to someone just starting out in group.

Notes:

So that the students feel totally free to say anything, the group facilitator and mentors are not present in the room for this focus group.

A summary of this evaluation can be found in the section titled "Insights and Reflections."

SESSION 14, 15, 16:
Preparation for Book-Signing Event

Focus:

• Students will name feelings and identify positive responses to those feelings.

• Students will develop organizational skills to plan an event. This event will allow them to share their writings with significant others.

• Students will develop public speaking skill.

Tasks: Week 14, 15, 16

1. Review group rules.

2. Each week the "feeling tree" is placed on the table and students choose a leaf to express their current feeling.

3. The facilitator suggests to the students that their writings and drawings be compiled into a booklet, and a "book-signing event" be planned. After this idea is explained, the students then move to different sections of the room with their mentors to brainstorm on proposed book titles. These proposed titles are then listed on the board and each student votes on her/his choice.

4. The facilitator discusses the program for the "book-signing event" with the students. The group agrees to the following:

• A student and mentor will give a brief welcoming speech to all present.

• Another student and mentor will give a brief explanation of the logistics for the event (all present will receive a copy of the book; each student reads one of their writings; students invite guests to bring their book for signing; guests can get their refreshments).

• A third student and mentor will give a brief explanation of what they learned and appreciated about the group.

• A fourth student and mentor will thank all involved in the group process and all in attendance at the event.

5. Each student and mentor takes strips of paper and writes some of the positive benefits of the group. One statement is written on each strip of paper. These strips of paper are then compiled into a paper chain that is to be used as a decoration at the book-signing event.

6. A worksheet is created to generate a commitment from each student to participate in the book-signing event. Then the students draw a slip of paper informing them of their role (the roles are listed in point 4 above) in the program, and they complete the worksheet *(See Appendix A)*.

7. The entire next session is used to rehearse the event.

SESSION 17: Gratitude

Focus:

• Students will name feelings and identify positive responses to those feelings.

• Students will name their thoughts and feeling about the book-signing event.

• Students will identify and name things for which they are grateful.

Tasks: Week 17

1. Review group rules.

2. The "feeling tree" is placed on the table and students choose a leaf to express their current feeling.

3. Students are asked to share their feelings about the book signing. They can respond to such things as: what made them feel proud—what did they enjoy—what do they want to remember—was there anything that surprised them.

4. The facilitator shares with the group her gratitude to each of the students for making the event successful. She explains that today we will talk about gratitude. A small bouquet of paper flowers is place in the center of the table. One by one each student is asked to pick a flower and say something for which they are grateful. The facilitator explains that being grateful and noticing the small things for which we are grateful can keep us focused and positive in our relations with others. Students are encouraged to give their flower to someone to whom they want to thank.

5. Students move to various sections of the room with their mentor to design a "Gratitude Coat of Arms" *(See Appendix A)*.

6. When students have completed the activity, they each stand and share with the group the meaning of the pictures they drew in their coat of arms.

SESSION 18:
Remembering and Staying Connected

Focus:

• Students will name feelings and identify positive responses to those feelings.

• Students will identify positive things they want to remember about the group process and about their connection to each other.

Tasks: Week 18

1. Review group rules.

2. The "feeling tree' is placed on the table and students choose a leaf to express their current feeling.

3. The students will play a game similar to hot potato. The facilitator will start by gently tossing a ball of yarn to one of the students. That student then says one thing he/she wants to remember about the group. That student then tosses the yarn to another and so on until all have had a chance to express what they want to remember. The piece of yarn has, in the process, provided a visual to show how they have been and are connected through being a part of the group. The facilitator explains this to the group.

4. The facilitator invites the students and their mentors to again complete the evaluation form *(See Appendix B)*.

5. The facilitator then explains that this is the last day for the group and that we want to stay connected as a group. In order to do this, small gift bags are placed on the table (one for each of the students). In each bag is a list of the names and phone numbers of all in the group, some pictures taken during the group process and book signing, a simple snack, an extra copy of the book they wrote titled "Shining in the Night," and some bookmarks *(See Appendix A)*.

6. Each student then receives their gift bag.

✓ Moving Forward

Insights and Reflections

Research on resiliency tells us that for children exposed to multiple risks, like the children of incarcerated parents, several factors stand out in those who develop successfully. The first factor recognizes the importance of attachment and predictable caring relationships for children and families. The second factor is to provide these children with activities and skill building opportunities that enhance self-esteem, and strengthen confidence and competence (Ann Adalist-Estrin). Those two factors became the backdrop for the activities and interactions planned for the students in this group process.

At the beginning of the group process, students were paired with a college-aged mentor who had successfully lived through the experience of parental incarceration. These mentors developed a deep relationship with their student partners as they engaged in the group process and activities. Additionally, the process was geared to provide group activities that enabled the students to identify their feelings, learn appropriate behaviors, and engage in skill building activities that fostered their self esteem and confidence. Thus, we were continually focused on resiliency. Murphy and Moriarty (*Vulnerability, Coping and Growth, Murphy and Moriarty*, Yale University Press, 1976) describe a resilient child as one who is "above all, an active, humorous, confident, and competent child who is prepared to take risks, although not unrealistic; who can alter his/her approach flexibly and, as a result of repeated successful coping experiences, has reason to feel confident of both inner and outer resources." The group activities and processes used by Let's Start were aimed at fostering resiliency in each of the children in the group.

An Evaluation of the Process Follows:

Pre- and post-tests on behavior showed little difference in the behavior of the children. However, historical data illustrated that between the group members, there were three principal visits and suspensions in the 2008–09 school year; these incidents were reduced to zero in the 2009–10 school year.

Because so many variables were at play during this process it is difficult to determine the exact impact of each intervention. However, we do know that the group members enjoyed and looked forward to coming to group each week. We also know that the group members indicated that the group was helpful and they had learned something from their discussions and activities: e.g., "I learned not to hit people if they say mean things about me," "I learned to express feelings without anger or jumping to conclusions—just because my dad is in jail, doesn't mean I have to be," "I learned how to keep secrets (confidences) and it's not okay to tell other people's business to my friends," "I used to get in trouble with my mom for talking about my daddy, but she took me to visit him in prison this semester."

The book-signing event was a major highlight of this process. It enabled the children to express some of the challenges, insights and dreams that they were experiencing through writing and art. Seeing their work in print—in a beautiful booklet titled "Shining in the Night"—engendered a feeling of pride and self worth in the students. The event itself, attended by the district superintendent, some school board members, the principal, teachers, family, and friends, allowed the students to realize, at least in the moment, that they indeed were talented, poised, and competent.

The current challenge faced by Let's Start is to develop a creative process to continue the mutually beneficial relationship established between the students and their mentors in the future.

In *Once Upon a Time When We Were Colored* (Clifton L. Taulbert, 1989), a young man leaving his home in Mississippi recounts the people in his life who provided relationships that made a difference—who protected him from risk. He listed his grandparents, a teacher, a neighbor, an uncle, and "my mother, who did not raise me but loved me as if she had." It is the hope of Let's Start that we, through the activities and relationships formed through this group process, will be amongst those special people listed by the children in this group. It is also the hope of Let's Start that the group discussions and activities enabled the students to develop and practice skills that will allow them to better cope with the stress and chaos that will inevitably be a part of their lives. It is the hope of Let's Start that each student will remember the words written by one of them:

"I shine bright even in the darkest night."

Appendix A
In-Group Handouts, by Session

SESSION 1:
Self Introduction

Self Introduction

Name:_____

Nickname:_____

Favorite food:_____

Favorite game:_____

Favorite TV show:_____

Favorite music:_____

Something that always makes me mad is:_____

_____

Something that always makes me laugh is:_____

_____

I am special because:_____

_____

SESSION 2:
Stories about My Parent

1. I always knew my mother was in prison, but at a certain point in my life I actually came to understand what that meant. It meant that my mother had made a bad decision and was being punished for it. Strangely, that embarrassed me. My feelings about embarrassment are hard to explain, but I was ashamed. I kept it a secret for a long time. Due to many conversations with family members and my Girl Scout troop, I finally stopped trying to hide the truth. And most people responded in a way that made me feel foolish for ever being embarrassed. They didn't look at me like I was crazy or stop being my friend. Most relationships didn't change, but I did lose one friend. After one of my friends found out about my mother being in prison, she told her mother, and her mother refused to let her hang out with me. No child should ever be punished for the wrong behavior of their parent.

2. My mother had been in and out of jail since before I was born, so her being in jail was nothing new to me. It wasn't really hard for me to disguise the fact that she was in jail because I had a great stepmother who always acted as a mother. The first time that I actually remember letting someone know that my mom was in jail, outside of my closest friends and family, was in high school. I was being filmed for a documentary and everyone wanted to know what it was for. I told them that it was because my mother was in prison. Everyone was surprised. Nobody knew; people thought my stepmother was my biological mother. From that moment on, I went all over St. Louis giving speeches on how to cope with the absence of a mother. I would say that I started out keeping my mom being in prison secret, but her being in prison turned out to be something very helpful.

3. The day I found out my mom went to prison, I was devastated. I didn't know what prison was because I was only five years old. I knew it was a place that took my mother away from me. I didn't know that if you did a bad thing, that was the place they send you. My mom made the decision to be on drugs, and that took away her freedom. Because my mom went to prison, she also lost the chance to see me and my sister grow up. I felt sad knowing I wasn't going to see my mom again until I was ten. I also started to feel angry because she left me. I didn't understand why anyone would leave their child/children behind. When my mom was in prison, I didn't share that anger with anyone but my sister. She was the only person I would really talk with about my mom being in prison, because that was something we had in common. All the other kids in school had their moms and dads at home, so what could they tell me? My mom is home now and our relationship is still topsy-turvy. I still hold a bit of resentment inside. I'm working on myself to let that go, because I don't want to be a bitter person who holds grudges.

SESSION 3:
Feeling Word Search Activity

c	g	d	a	s	h	o	m	d	l
o	r	u	s	c	a	r	e	d	a
n	d	y	h	o	p	e	c	f	p
f	r	h	a	p	p	y	l	u	n
u	c	o	m	s	a	f	o	r	f
s	a	f	e	p	h	r	v	e	r
e	m	a	d	y	g	i	e	l	I
d	o	d	e	a	o	s	a	d	e
l	m	v	o	l	d	r	g	s	n
p	r	I	s	o	n	l	e	d	d

Words:

Happy	Confused	Friend
Mad	Mom	Love
Sad	Dad	Cry
Ashamed	Group	Hope
Scared	Prison	Me

SESSION 4:
Think Before You Act

_____

_____

_____

_____

WRITING ACTIVITIES
Sessions 6, 7, 8

WRITING ACTIVITY 1

We are going to write a short poem about "Me, Myself and I."

Make it a two-line poem that says something about you. Before you write, talk with your mentor to decide what you want to say and to figure out a rhyme. Here are two examples:

Me, Myself and I . . .

I'm cute, Black, intelligent, and clean.

No monster in this whole world can make me mean.

Or

My name is Jackie, and I'm a teacher.

I'm not like any other creature.

NOW, write your poem about YOU

_____

_____

_____

_____

WRITING ACTIVITY 1 cont'd.

NOW, write about how you are special. Talk with your mentor before you begin writing. Write at least 5 things that make you special. Begin each sentence with: I am special because . . .

_____

_____

_____

_____

_____

_____

_____

_____

_____

_____

Let's do one more writing about YOU. Tell us the many things that make you special. Here are some examples:

- I am special because I am clever.

- I am special because I am Black.

- I am special because I care for people.

- I am special because those who hurt me I will pray for.

- I am special because I know how to ignore IGNORANCE.

_____

_____

_____

_____

_____

_____

_____

_____

WRITING ACTIVITY 2

This writing activity will focus on the choices you make. To begin, we will make a list of some of the choices you make every day. Here are some examples:

- I choose to do my work.

- I choose to listen to my teachers, my parents, and my elders.

- I choose to be kind to my sister.

- I choose to not fight.

NOW, you make your list of choices. Talk with your mentor before you begin. Begin each sentence with: I choose to . . .

_____

_____

_____

_____

_____

_____

_____

Write a short story and call it: *I Can Change*. Here are two examples:

I CAN CHANGE

I think I can change, and if I change I can be a good man and an intelligent boy. I think I can change if I do the right things. The right things are:

- To be in school every day.

- To be on time so I will not miss the bus.

- To stop fights when I see them.

- To walk away when somebody calls me a name.

Or

Your story could be something like this:

My name is Jane, and I want to change. Sometimes in school, the other kids make fun of me. When that happens, I can walk away. My sister is fussy, and I can change if I am patient and kind to her. My teacher says I can do better work, especially in math. I can change by studying hard and doing my homework.

WRITING ACTIVITY 2 cont'd.

NOW, write your story. Talk with your mentor before you start writing.

WRITING ACTIVITY 3

WHAT IS HAPPY AND WHAT IS SAD

Write two paragraphs, one about what makes you sad and one about what makes you happy. Here are some examples:

- I was sad when my uncle got locked up.

- I was sad when my bike was stolen.

- I was very sad when my brother got locked up.

- I was sad when my grandmother died. We talked about her and what she did for us.

NOW, write about what makes you sad. Talk about it with your mentor first.

_____

_____

_____

NOW, write about what makes you happy. Talk about it with your mentor first.

_____

_____

_____

WRITING ACTIVITY 4

Write a story about what makes you mad or angry. Talk with your mentor before writing. Explain the situation, then state your choices.

For example, you could say:

> What makes me angry is when people talk about me. One time . . . (tell what happened). Here is what I did. . . . Another choice is . . .

NOW write your story:

_____

_____

_____

_____

_____

NOW, make a list of some kind things you did this past week.

_____

_____

_____

_____

WRITING ACTIVITY 5

Role Models:

Who is a role model for you? Talk about this with your mentor. Talk about your role model and why you respect and want to be like this person.

NOW, write about your role model. Tell who it is and the reasons you look up to this person.

_____

_____

_____

_____

_____

_____

_____

_____

_____

WRITING ACTIVITY 6

My Family

Write a story that begins with the sentence: My dad is in prison. Then, write whatever you want. Talk with your mentor before you write.

_____

_____

_____

_____

_____

_____

_____

_____

_____

_____

_____

_____

WRITING ACTIVITY 7

My Dreams

Write about some of your dreams or your wishes for yourself. Talk with your mentor before you write. Begin your writing with the statement: I dream . . .

_____

_____

_____

_____

_____

_____

_____

_____

_____

SCENARIOS
Sessions 6, 7, 8

Latasha got a letter from her dad who is in prison. He told her he has to stay there for five more years.

*****

Willie just got an A on a math test.

*****

Lucy's friend wants her to go with her to the store to steal some candy. "It's only candy," she says.

*****

Donald got in trouble in class. Then he got in a fight. He thinks he will end up in prison just like his dad.

*****

Ronnell got first place in his spelling bee at school.

*****

Brittany told her mom she was going to her friend's house. Instead, she went to the mall to meet someone her mom does not want her to see.

*****

Raheem's teacher feels that he is being disruptive in class. But he feels his teacher is picking on him.

*****

Sherice got a phone call from her dad in prison.

*****

Kayla sees her brother using an illegal drug.

*****

Joan overhears some kids talking mean about one of the kids who is in a special group with her.

*****

Donnel's mom tells him they are going to visit his dad in prison.

*****

Torre sees two older boys grab the lunch from a younger boy as they are walking to school.

*****

Session 16:
Book-Signing Worksheet

1. I would like to participate in this book-signing event   YES   NO

2. I will do my part to make the event a good one.   YES   NO

3. What are two specific things I will do for this event?

4. Who will I invite (you may invite two adults and two friends)?

5. Refreshments: We will have home-made cookies. Make two or three other suggestions:

6. Write your speech here (you and your mentor can share it):

SESSION 17:
Gratitude

SESSION 18:
Bookmark

Let's Start
with the Kids
University City, MO

Appendix B
Sample Forms and Surveys

NOTE: All evaluation forms used were the same as in year 1.

Appendix C
Additional Resources

Saint Louis Region Resources:
Let's Start Caregivers Resource Guide
Big Brothers Big Sisters Amachi Program
Girl Scouts Behind Bars
Coalition for Children of Offenders
MO 4-H LIFE Program

Information and Online Resources:
Family Corrections Network
Center for Children of Incarcerated Parents
Bureau of Justice Statistics

The movie *When the Bough Breaks* is a documentary by Jill Evans Petzall
& Deeds Rogers. ©2001 Beacon Productions, Inc. It is a presentation of
the Independent Television Service (ITVS).

Let's Start with the Kids wishes to acknowledge and graciously thank all of the individuals who worked on this handbook, its processes, and group facilitation:

Stacey Miller, MSW, LCSW
Liz Downey, MSW
Erin Whitham, MSW
Niquija Burns, MSW
Jillian Palacios
Roosevelt Roberts
Taylor Shelton
Donna Zuroweste, MBA
Jackie Toben, SSND

CPSIA information can be obtained at www.ICGtesting.com
Printed in the USA
LVOW040905080212

267705LV00002B/9/P

9 781933 370989